HOW to NOt
ALWAYs Be WORKiNg

HOW to NOt ALWAYS BE WORKiNG

A toolkit for creativity and radical self-care

MARLee GRACe

MORROW GIFT

AN IMPRINT OF WILLIAM MORROW

HarperCollins books may be purchased for educational, business, or sales promotional use. For information please email the Special Markets Department at SPsales@harpercollins.com.

FIRST EDITION

Designed by Leah Carlson-Stanisic
Illustrations by Rob Moss Wilson

Library of Congress Cataloging-in-Publication Data has been applied for.

ISBN 978-0-06-280367-2

23   IM   10 9 8 7 6 5

For

JACQUELINE & ANDREW,

in unconditional &

cosmic support

INTRODUCTION; or, the ONLY RULE is WORK

Here is a book, a workbook, a guide, an ode to not knowing. I wrote it first as a tiny zine that I typed up on my typewriter. I glued all the words down and scanned in the pages, printed them out, and stapled them together. I wrote it for myself. The more I shared the little workbook with other people, the more I found that my friends were also in deep need of this process of identifying our work.

Learning how to not always be working isn't about working less or never working or never having a job. It's about starting to personally determine for one's self the concept of work. To ask the questions: *Why does it matter? What does it mean? How do you always show up for yourself?*

Hint: It's all work, the only rule is work. This is working, the diving in. And it feels so good. It is a gift, and my gratitude overflows that typing this very introduction is indeed my work.

I made a decision to be my own boss at some point, but it was sort of an accident. I mean, I've always been pretty bossy (I'm a big sister, a performer, a manifester of sorts), so it wasn't a far leap to be my own boss. But with a BFA in dance and no real business training or, hell, any training on being a person, I started to really sink. Well, not sink, but like not tread and not swim. I would sort of do the butterfly and then the breaststroke and be really good at them, then all of a sudden find myself on my back looking at the sky in utter appreciation with water entering my ears. It was like being in a dream but also being afraid that if I shifted, I might not remember how to swim again.

I actually took swimming lessons a few times and am pretty good at swimming. It is to this day my absolute favorite way to not work: to enter Tomales Bay or Lake Michigan and swim as far out as I can, no phone in hand, no to-do list (the words would smear, ya know), keeping the sadness at bay. It was the moment I thought, "What if I got a waterproof phone case? I could swim and work at the same time!" that I knew I had taken it too far (the working).

So here we are.

When I began thinking about this topic it was spring of 2015, and I was living in Michigan, married, and running a shop and artists' residency called Have Company. I had picked up knitting as a way to cope—with anxiety, depression, being a person in recovery, and generally being easily distracted.

Without much thought (that is generally how I make decisions—impulsiveness can be the truest way to express passion for being alive), I decided it would be a great idea to start selling yarn at Have Company. I reached out to a yarn company, ordered a ton of yarn, and then all of a sudden was facing a very big and weird problem. Selling yarn and knitting were now part of my job. I had turned this HOBBY that HEALS me into my WORK.

It didn't stop there. Every time I would sit down with my partner, I was working. I was checking email on my phone. When I was knitting, I was documenting the knitting and the quilting process. It was all part of my work. And in this case, when I say "work," I mean the way that I am generating income for my small business. My work consumed me in a way that was no longer giving me life, but I was obsessed and couldn't really see clearly what had gone wrong.

In the end, a few things shifted. My marriage ended, and I decided to close my space and move to California. I came to Oakland, a place I had many friends—but quickly knew it was not my home. I traveled north to Point Reyes to go for a hike one day and immediately knew it was where I wanted to land, and I am so grateful to call this rural place my home. That day, I drove by a cow giving birth. The calf slipped out of its mother, and it was the sweetest invitation for me to slow down, pay better attention, and nest here.

I write this as a twenty-nine-year-old, on the brink of the peak of my Saturn return. Today I ate breakfast with my partner and told them a hundred fears I have about WHO WILL I BE when this document comes out in a year. I am filled with fear, but the point is, I still show up and I still make things. It isn't that the fear goes away. They might not be my partner in a year; I might not live in California—there is no knowing. And that is the greatest gift: the groundlessness.

Becoming my own boss was the best thing I ever decided to do and also the hardest. I mostly do whatever I want whenever I want to and don't have anyone telling me what to do. But I'm also completely and totally on my own, with no safety net and only myself to fall back on. And sometimes that's a scary thing. I can slip into patterns of dishonoring myself: ignoring bills, overworking one side of my business and not paying enough attention to the other, forgetting that exercise is a thing, depleting my body with too much refined sugar, ignoring emails for weeks, taking great cell phone pictures but producing no blog posts or real meat to go with them.

This book isn't just for folks who are their own boss. It is for everyone who wants to understand the different categories of their life. And for people who hate categories and want to tell me it's all just the same, this book is for you, too. It's just a book, it's just a thing I made, really. You can read it with a friend, you can give it to a friend.

This is for people with a nine-to-five who come home and can't seem to close their computers, for the nurse who picks up every single extra shift so she doesn't have to face self-care and ritual. It's for anyone who is using work or tasks or habits as a way of escaping their truest self, which, if you ask me, is making something: a home, a baby, a recipe, a shop, an installation, a new dance, a blanket.

Much of my work and research as an artist and a dancer are led by the words of women: Julia Cameron and Angeles Arrien. Both of these women's writings about being an artist, the tarot, cross-cultural studies, and showing up in a radical and wild way guide me in my own path. Although I never met Angeles while she was alive, I am grateful to have mentors who passed down her work. Two other books that have had a great impact on me as I wrote this one were *Emergent Strategy* by Adrienne Maree Brown and *How to Be*

Bored by Eva Hoffman. I am just so endlessly grateful for others who are putting in the work and research on how our lives exist in this digital age, which is so chaotic and dizzying at times.

This book is a labor of yes. A labor of saying yes to the process, a labor of showing up, taking time, taking a time-out. You can read it all in one go and take notes. You can fill its blank areas with your own lists. I included a lot of my own lists and asked some of my friends for some of theirs, too. Hanging out with my friends even when we are sort of working is my greatest way to not work. I mean, it's a gray area, but it's human and makes me feel whole and not so disconnected. My phone screen—that tends to disconnect me.

So put your phone away. Turn it off or put it on airplane mode. Having a screen-free experience while you navigate this book could prove to be really powerful. Each time I have sat down to write, I have turned mine off or put it across the room. I tried to keep it close by (ya know, for the time and in case of emergency?!) but that wasn't working, so I bought a watch.

Get a watch. And an alarm clock. And a disposable camera. Those are your first three tasks. Then you won't need your phone. You can put it in a room that is not your bedroom at night so that when your eyes open you don't just start working. Find these objects at a thrift store, or maybe you have them in your basement.

A lot of this navigating is about how to exist within capitalism in a feminine and a feminist way. Not a female way, but in a softer way, exploring a more tender approach to running a business or just existing in the world than the patriarchy condones. You don't need to buy anything to be a witch, to have an altar. The earth is your tool. Water, air, fire, and earth are free. We are here to walk gently among the seasons and the resources she gives us: but to build an altar you just need a rock and a stick, ya know.

So although in the book I will suggest tools that would require some sort of purchasing, I encourage you to engage the resources that are already around you whenever possible.

A note on privilege: We are living in a time and a world and in a country where we are not all able to access the same things because of systematic racism, the patriarchy, capitalism, and so much more. It is important to know that this book was written from my perspective as a white, queer, cis, able-bodied woman. This is my experience, and a lot of privilege is inherent in my body and being.

It is my hope that by including the voices of many of my friends and peers, who span a much broader demographic, that the book can speak to anyone who is drawn to a radical way of existing and working. My hope for this book is that it offers an entryway for a number of folks at the crossroads of work and career and life and aliveness. Whether you are a booming business owner and really can't stop, or you are working minimum wage and can't seem to get ahead: I see you, and I know these feelings on both ends. There are a lot of feelings I don't know as well, but I offer my words as a starting point for myself and anyone holding this.

I write in the hope of manifesting a more balanced way of navigating these topics for all of us, especially those who have less access and fewer opportunities. I offer these words as a hope and as a manifestation that rest and leisure and deep breathing are for everyone, not just the 1%, not just the enlightened, not just the privileged; they are for anyone who has two minutes. This book is not about self-care for the self, but self-care for the collective and liberation from the obsession of work.

This book is for anyone who is
looking to show up to their life, this one
true journey of being alive.

CHAPTER 1

WHAt is My WORK?

The best way you can create healthy boundaries around work is to get clear about what your work actually is. For me, usually if it feels hard I think it's work, and if it feels easy I assume it is not work. And this is not only untrue, but is also part of why I am showing up to write these pages. Your work is not the same thing as your job, but sometimes it can be. Often, I get paid for jobs that feel easy and don't feel like work, then I do a bunch of them and implode, burning out because I accidentally forgot I was working. I forgot to take a walk. I forgot to take a break. I forgot that I don't have to share with the world every tiny thing that I do.

For some of us, that is our work—sharing every tiny thing that we do. Every tiny beach trip, every tiny victory, every tiny moment. So it would seem that if our eyes are open, we are most likely working . . . and most likely forgetting to breathe, forgetting to drink water, forgetting to forgive ourselves for forgetting.

Work is not bad. Always working is not a bad thing, if that's your intention.

I have this voice in my head who loves to tell me I'm not doing a good enough job, or that working all the time is a terrible idea. I named the voice Roger. This helped me identify this voice and separate it out, so I could sort of address it, like, "Hey, Roger, thanks so much for stopping by today and giving your input, but I am actually all set."

I also just love working! It not only lets me shut down Roger, but it makes me feel great. I love to get things done, and I love to work, and I love to work next to other people who are working, and I love when my friends are deeply dedicated to their art making practices and small businesses.

And when you love something, it can be extremely hard to tell if you're working. For example, gardening is absolutely not working to me. But if I share it on the internet, I am getting into some tricky territory. (Oh, look, a tiny moment where I am gardening, or I picked some kale—most likely kale that I didn't plant, but I picked it and I showed everyone—so now is it part of my work?)

If you are a professional gardener and you are so into gardening and you are growing vegetables and selling them at the farmers' market, then gardening very well might be on your work list. Maybe you make zero dollars gardening but it feels like work to you. (Wait, actually, if I really did garden it would feel like work, so that's probably why I don't do it.)

See what I mean? Do you see what I'm getting at? There is no real answer, it's all work. It's also all not work. Work is subjective. I do, however, know that when the things on my work list became the only things I was doing, it hurt my spirit, my partnership, my friendships, and my business. Always working proved to be completely unsustainable for my mental health and also for those around me. So I set out on this mission to correct this and am happy to report that by bringing in just the awareness, just a willingness to be aware, much growth has happened. You honestly don't even have to practice awareness, you just have to simply be willing to be aware. Through this, my relationship with working has begun its healing process.

In order to cultivate some sort of definition of working vs. not working, you have to start somewhere. So start with a list. *Your* list.

..ıⅷⓘ‖ıₗₗ

CHAPTER 1 EXERCISES

THIS IS MY WORK

Use the space below to identify the tasks you perform that are work. Before you start:

Take a deep breath and know that this list is ever changing.
Make yourself some herbal tea or coffee, something that makes you feel good and relaxed.

Now write your list.

_____

_____

_____

_____

_____

_____

_____

_____

_____

HERE IS WHAT WORKING IS TO ME

- Answering emails
- Balancing the books
- Unlocking the front door to the shop
- Ringing someone up at the cash register
- Managing my online shop (inventory, etc.)
- Blogging
- Uploading a new podcast episode
- Organizing classes and workshops and adding them to the website and Facebook
- Basically anything that involves a computer
- Posting to Instagram about a new product or service
- Sending out a newsletter
- Sweeping and mopping my workspace
- Business development/reevaluation

HOW TO LOVE ADMIN/BUSYWORK/ PAPERWORK—THE STUFF THAT IS *NOT* CREATIVE OR FUN—AND GET IT DONE

I have learned a lot from increasing my ability to withstand cardio. At first I dreaded the work. It felt stressful throughout each workout, and yet the endorphins and energy post-workout left a hint of something good and the motivation to come back and try again. Eventually the feeling of dread before I started subsided. I learned how to prepare for each workout (hydrate, eat protein an hour before, eat quickly after, do a recovery workout the next day, etc.), and the reward of strength, a faster recovery, and the joy of the process took over. I learned techniques for preparing, got good at the tasks, and enjoyed the feeling of accomplishment.

This is the same process for admin/busywork/paperwork. I don't love updating my books and accounting, but I built the skills and systems so it doesn't feel like a struggle anymore. I follow a routine to enjoy it (see: chocolate, music, podcasts, etc.), and the feeling of accomplishment keeps me coming back without dread. I want to like my work, so I master it. It can be a relief to listen to music, sip on a chai latte, and just plug away at my accounting. When I feel distracted, I think of the results over the process and try to get back to it.

I also limit the time I spend on administrative work. It shouldn't take all day. What's more frustrating than spending the whole day dreading and avoiding, when the task takes only ten minutes? There are a billion other things I would rather do than avoid the work.

Last, but certainly not least, I remind myself that I am always in progress and, thus, so is my work. I fine-tune my tools every day and know that some days I will be stronger than others.

—SARAH SCHULWEIS, BUSINESS CONSULTANT

> For me, I have more or less made the decision to define work as my job. However, my job description includes tasks that are not on my work list, but will show up later.

WHAT IS MY WORK? AN EXPANSION EXERCISE

Now that you have this simple list written, take some time to consider it. Look at each item and expand on *why* it is your work. Is it because it is hard? Because it makes you money? Because you would prefer not to do it?

Once you clarify this for yourself, you can get a better picture of which tasks and jobs you might want to learn to love or which ones you might want to delegate.

Delegating is cool: delegating provides other people jobs and empowering tasks, and delegating gives you more time to do the work that brings you wild and great joy.

_____

_____

_____

_____

_____

Your work might be "painting every morning" and your job description might be "being a radical parent to my homeschooled children"—and those things might not generate any income for you. Or your job/work could be being a blogger who makes their living off of sharing their life as a homeschooling parent . . .

My point is both are all still work. Even better, now that you've identified these areas, you can start to navigate them in a way that is a little softer, a little more meaningful.

Be soft on yourself, be tender with your spirit. This isn't easy, it's work. It is absolutely work for me to look at myself, to look at my patterns and my habits and my ways of being. The work _is_ the process; they are interchangeable. On the other side of this work, though, is freedom, lightness. After all, it's lighter than you think.

To close, I'll have you write out why you are grateful for your work. This will help us continue to navigate the book with a sense of gratitude—because, after all, the simple fact that this is what we are grappling with is a real gift.

I am grateful for . . .
- The freedom to make my own schedule
- The people who have come into my life through running a shop
- The skills I have learned by teaching them to myself
- The skills I have learned from others, especially through barter or trade
- The internet—although I have problems with self-control (see chapter 5). I am grateful for all the web has given me in terms of connections with real live people

What about your work are you grateful for?

_____

_____

_____

_____

_____

CHAPTER 2

WHERE DO I WORK?

So now that you have identified what your work is, what does your workspace look like? Is it okay to work on the couch? Do you feel powerful on the couch? Is the dining room table the best place for you, or when it's time for dinner are you overwhelmed because you are now eating in your workspace? Or maybe you love eating in your workspace; then the dining room table is your church of work. Can you get a tiny table? Where is your tiny table? Set your tiny table up like an altar.

These examples are mostly for the freelancer, but many of you also have a desk in a cubicle or an office. A space that is not your own and belongs to someone else can still be filled with the same charm and magic as a space in your home. Bringing in crystals, plants, a small art print or collage you've made, and other items that invoke a sense of creativity and positive space.

Again, there is no right or wrong way to inhabit your work environment. There is no wrong way to have a sacred workspace. There is only your way and that's why we are writing, to find it and to celebrate it.

AN IDEAL WORKSPACE FOR A KNITTER
Brandi Harper

My ideal workspace has white walls with lavender accents. Lots of green plants and indoor trees. There's a chair to knit in. Sheep's wool, beach stones, and lots of works in progress alongside finished works.

A question I am forever asking myself is: "Do I want my workspace to be in my home or would I like an outside office/studio?"

It has been beneficial to me to have a separate space that is an art studio, a place that is a dance studio, and a place that is an office space for admin work/shipping. But I am also a real and true believer in the dining room table as the workspace table, eating table, creative space table—with designated places for the materials to live.

The dining room table/neutral space as workspace, with designated places for materials to live, can look so many different ways. I really love a good mobile art cart and a shelf where the research goes. And, of course, a good basket can do the trick.

I love baskets. Don't even get me started on how much I love a good basket. Thrift stores are overflowing with baskets. Free piles, clothing swaps, thrift stores—baskets galore. I am really bad at organizing. Like really, really not good at it. I am sort of at this place in my life where I am honoring the duality of "How can I get better at physical organization?" and "How can I also just sort of accept that I am a tornado person?"

Twyla Tharp talks about having a physical box for every project. That way, as you research and think about the project, you can add things to the box as you go: notes you write yourself, newspaper clippings that inspire you about the project, etc.

You could make a Google Docs box or that sort of thing. A folder, a Pinterest board! People use Pinterest. I always forget about Pinterest, and then I remember.

Maybe a bulletin board, the original Pinterest.

To sum up: Never let someone tell you that you *have* to have it be a certain way. I have written parts of this book at a loud coffee shop, on an airplane, in my bed, on a couch, in my old store, in my friend's office, at my dining room table, at my parents' dining room table . . . the list goes on.

Note: Every time I write, there was an altar. And everything and anything can be an altar. Nine out of ten times this is a physical altar, but there have been times when it has been a metaphorical altar.

CHAPTER 2 EXERCISE

In the space below, write out your dream workspace. It can truly be whatever YOUR dream is, not what you think it should be. What comes up for you intuitively? From plants, to paint colors, to table size.

_____

_____

_____

_____

_____

_____

_____

_____

_____

Now take a look at some of the questions below and jot down your answers on these pages.

Do I have easy access to taking breaks in my current workspace? What are actions I could take to set up my space in a way that supports me?

_____

_____

What can I add to my current workspace to make it more comfortable, sacred, and encouraging? (Examples: a teakettle and your favorite teas, a chair that supports your lower back.)

_____

_____

Can I take breaks within my current workspace for stretches? (Tip: Add a yoga mat!)

_____

_____

Does my current workspace have a rug or other objects that turn it into a cozier space?

_____

_____

CHAPTER 3

WHAt is NOt My WORK?

We're about to get real free, and we're not even halfway there. Identifying what is *not* your work can be one of the most powerful things you can do for yourself. I'm not just making that up—see, I made a list and was immediately freer.

○ ○ ○

WHAT IS NOT MY WORK?

- Card games: Dutch Blitz, Egyptian Rat Screw, Cards Against Humanity
- Eating dinner
- Making herbal infusions
- New moon circles

- Watching TV shows
- Going for a walk
- Sitting on the beach (ouch . . . see chapter 4 for this one)
- Meditation
- Reading
- Being intimate with a partner
- Taking a bath (or a shower, but I mean *come onnnn*, amen baths)
- Listening to a podcast (and not multitasking)
- Lying on the couch and listening to a record (and not multitasking)
- Not multitasking
- CAMPING!
- Nature, adventure, etc.
- Doing this whole list without a phone or computer in sight
- Getting a tattoo
- Eating pie

In considering this list, I have identified that a large part of both my "job" and my "work" is sharing many moments of my personal life, that people are drawn to my shop/artists' residency because I share the not-so-glamorous details of bumpin' along in my process of healing and creating and living. I'm grateful for this, deep in my bones. *But* it also means I need to ask: Where is my time? What does it mean to not work?

For me, that last line is the key: when I am not sharing is when I am not working. That means putting my phone *away*. Even when I record the podcast with each resident, I take their photograph with a Polaroid camera. I want it to not feel so digital, our time together.

My rituals and reveries in the morning are also an invaluable part of my not working. On a good day, I don't turn on my phone or computer until ten A.M. This is certainly not possible every day. And if you are a person whose *best* work hours on a phone or computer are seven A.M. to ten A.M., then this is no good for you either. Who knows, maybe those are my best work hours too. Alas, I have been experimenting with a strict NO PHONE rule from ten P.M. to ten A.M., and it has been pretty magical. Even if I wake up to meet someone for a work-oriented meeting at nine A.M., I still try to stick to my phone rule. If those hours don't work for you, I suggest you find some that do!

MY RITUALS BEFORE TEN A.M.

- Open eyes, turn alarm off—do not hit snooze (don't worry, I still hit snooze sometimes and then have to try really hard to forgive myself for it).

- Roll out of bed onto a sweet little carpet my friend Megan made and say my prayers (to the spirit of the universe/eternal goddess of the earth) and express gratitude for my life. Sometimes I even say a li'l prayer for anyone bothering me, praying they find healing.

- Meditate for ten minutes. (Not into ten? Try one. Not impressed with my ten? Do an hour, I know you can.)

- Daily reflection book (reading). I prefer a good, powerful (and def a li'l cheesy) book by Melody Beattie, author of *Codependent No More*. *The Language of Letting Go* daily reflection book is my personal favorite.

- Morning pages (writing). Dear Julia Cameron, thank you for this gift to humankind. Morning pages are from the book *The Artist's Way* and are simply three pages of free writing first thing in the mornin'.

- Make coffee! Or drink coffee someone else made me. Sometimes this happens more or less at the same time as morning pages.

- I might light a few candles, although this tends to be more part of my nighttime rituals.

○ ○ ○

SOME WORDS ON EVENINGS
AND NOT WORKING BY SARAH SCHULWEIS

At this point in my life, I dedicate my evenings to being "work" free. By the time I get to four P.M., I'm unable to concentrate or contribute in a valuable way, and I move on to do the work of recovering. Some people protect their mornings, some midday. It doesn't matter when as long as you know when your alone or recovery time is and protect it. This understanding means that you know when you concentrate best and work around that so you can recover during hours that aren't optimal. Or vice versa.

My only fully functional computer is in my office, so any work with clients has to be done in that space and finished by the time I leave that space. If it's not done, I don't assume or try to work on it at home. That helps me with time management on a weekly and daily basis. I don't think one needs an office or desktop computer, but limiting where and when you work is helpful. Just because you can take your computer anywhere doesn't mean you should.

.ıΙⓘⓘⓘⓘ..

CHAPTER 3 EXERCISE

ON WINDING DOWN; OR, HOW TO NOT WORK AFTER YOU'VE WORKED ALL DAY

There are still days where I work literally every minute of the day, partly because I love it, partly because I am a little obsessed sometimes, and often because I just forget to take breaks. This is why I enlisted the strict and nonnegotiable "No Work After Ten P.M." rule.

Write your own nighttime ritual here to help you decide what time you need to stop working.

_____

_____

_____

_____

_____

_____

_____

_____

I *love* the act of truly powering down. Not just airplane mode, not just a silent phone, but phone turned *off*. Before I started on this path of "phone healing," I think I maybe went literally an entire year without turning my phone off. It might be safe to say most of us never turn our phones off. I just got some chills. Turn it off.

I usually go to bed around 11:30 P.M., so an hour and a half feels like a nice amount of time for me to wind down. Sometimes I'll want to knit and watch a show during that time, but recently I have been staying committed to no screen time whatsoever, movie time included, unless watching with a friend or my partner or something. Then it might feel correct because I'm also connecting.

MY NIGHTTIME RITUALS

- Around 9:30 P.M. I start to remember I need to power down in thirty minutes, so I might shoot off one last text or email, make sure my morning plans are set in stone, and put my pajamas on.

- At 10 P.M. I power down completely. No phone on and no computer.

- From 10 to 11:30 P.M. I will make some tea and read usually. The gray area might swoop in, because I sure do love to read books about creativity and related to my work . . . Still, it is reading nonetheless, and it isn't a direct action that makes money, so it feels like positive winding down, not working time.

- I love a good bowl of ice cream at 10:30 P.M. :)
- This is also a great time to connect with a partner or roommates, anyone whom you share a home with. I was amazed how much my relationships improved when my body was wound down and my phone was put away.
- I have a candle-lighting ritual at night, with many different colors for different intentions (see list opposite). This helps me set goals and have a li'l nighttime prayer, expressing gratitude for my past twenty-four hours on earth.
- Crawl in bed. I might do a li'l more reading here and close my eyes. Oh, and turn the fan on. I am addicted to fan noises.

Not only do these actions help me wind down and wind back up in the morning, but they also keep me clear and more mindful throughout the day. If I skip my morning pages, I am way more apt to forget to take a break midday when I am stressed or overworking myself.

SIMPLE GUIDE FOR CANDLE COLORS

BLACK: Grounding, wisdom, learning, protection, repel negative energy

WHITE: Peace, truth

BLUE: Communication, focus, patience, truth, inspiration

LAVENDER: Intuition, healing

ORANGE: Joy, energy, creativity

SILVER: Feminine energy, psychic awareness, moon magic

BROWN: House blessing, concentration, earth magic

YELLOW: Pleasure, happiness

GREEN: Prosperity, abundance, money, growth

CHAPTER 4

WHAT ARE tHE gRAy AREAS iN MY WORK?

A s we continue to navigate these roles of what is a job and what is work, we need to keep in mind the point: to create balance—or, more important, to intend to create balance. When work begins to get in the way of balance, a radical notion of self-care, you may need a more thorough visual of what your work is.

Knitting is probably my biggest gray area. It is absolutely the best way for me to get out of my head, to relax, to forget about the day. But I also share it as part of carrying yarn in my shop. So I ask myself: Is one way to separate work to choose things to keep private. What if I didn't take a picture of every project, like a gift I'm making a friend. I can make it for them, send it, and feel the actual joy and satisfaction of them receiving it, without having to have anyone know about it. Sometimes sharing it is part of my work, and sometimes the cheap thrill of a few hundred likes lessens its value and simplicity. It only has to become work if I tell it to become work. Dear dishcloth, you are now work.

○ ○ ○

WORDS FROM JOSEY BAKER BREAD

I'm a bread baker. That feels so good to say! I'm a bread baker, and I love it! Not only do I love it, I just keep loving it more and more the deeper I get into the craft. How is this possible, you wonder? After seven years of baking, I've got more questions than answers, and every day provides me with ample opportunity to explore the unknown, practice patience and sensitivity, and make beautiful and delicious objects that bring people together. Not to mention the fact that I get to do it with and for a community that I feel deeply rooted within.

Yes, I feel so very lucky to be able to say that I love the thing I "am," a bread baker. By some wild stroke of luck I managed to turn my passion into my profession, and not a day goes by that I don't feel grateful for it. But the truth is these days I spend most of my time doing things other than baking bread. It's one of the consequences of small-business "success" that most people won't tell you—the more you succeed at your profession as it is, the less you engage with your passion as it was. But this isn't a bad thing. It's just an opportunity to evolve your passion and continue to grow and find beauty in places you never knew existed. I wonder what I'll find tomorrow.

A FEW WORDS ON WORK AS IN THE EVERYTHING BY ANGEL NAFIS

As a writer, my job is formally to be a really good noticer. Good poems require that I see what is going on around me and inside of me and trying to fasten my observations to words before they disappear. So in this way, I am always working. When I am on the Q train, when I am in the shower lathering my pits, when I'm arguing with my partner about whose turn it is to change the cat's litter, unfortunately/fortunately the poem is always right there, waiting for me to notice it. It can be overwhelming sometimes, especially for my personality type, which is exhaustively looking to maximize opportunity and move on to the next thing before I've finished the first. So to slow down and separate my work life from my "regular" life, I try to download my spontaneous creative thoughts to a nearby journal or the notes app in my phone. This helps get the thought or line of a poem out of the front of my brain and at the top of my attention and enables me to stay present to whatever task or moment I am in. And when the beauty is too potent and my heart too greedy for that to work, it is always helpful to remember that part of being a creative-based worker is knowing when to surrender to your instincts to make. Such surrendering can yield your most rewarding, surprising work. Like this poem I wrote yonder:

At the CRACKER BARREL in tewksbury, Massachusetts
(excerpts)

eACH ALARM A voice SAYing, if you HeRe, i'm HeRe.
BACK Home, the Blue - BLACK tRAin conductoR who winks
At me ANO HOLDS the DooRS AN extRA twenty seconds.
the CHestNUt BANKeR, who DeSpite HeR PinstRiPes
SNickeRS At my Jokes, ciRcles HeR NAme on the
CARD SHe HANDS Me. tHAt MAilMAN with the Locks,
who MADe Room foR me on the SiDewalk AND SAiD

I'm Not tRyNA BotheR you, i DoN't wANt to SCARe
you, but you ARe ReAlly somethiNg.

these RAMSHACKLe ANgels, SPRAwLing,
ANoNymous, woo - woo, Right on time.

There could be many gray areas in your own work, and in some ways the order of this chapter could stand to be switched with the one before it. Alas, looking at your day-to-day activities is a great place to start to see what gray areas exist for you.

A lot of the gray area for me can also be in my sharing of my rituals and survival/self-care practices. For instance, my ritual of going to the beach every Monday and sharing it on social media has become part of my, dare I say this word, "brand." When I go to the beach I do not feel as if I am at work, per se—that admin-style side of working. But it is my work to share my life and my process, and going to the beach every Monday is part of that.

Here are a few words from Nicole Lavelle, a designer and social practice artist whose work is deeply embedded in the forever noticing and being a part of. Her research and her work, for instance, were writing these words (but it is a gray area).

Nicole and I love going to the county fair together. She really values and explores concepts of leisure, relaxation, and communing with nature, both to visit and to find a home within it. Here are some reflections on relaxation time and how it can still feel like a form of work, requiring greater presence and attention:

It is difficult to be present completely. I find it rare that a leisure experience encompasses my attention, takes me entirely, is able to keep me from having planning thoughts or future-worry.

The fair is an exception. The fair is an encompassing experience. For me, there is a shift that happens as soon as I am finished purchasing my ticket from the person in the plywood kiosk and I step through the chain-link fence into a dusty, crowded fairgrounds in the summer.

The fair is overstimulating in the best way. It requires my entire attention span. It requires me to be present.[*]

Maybe my biggest gray area is this research on how to work better. Maybe that is really what I am trying to find through all of this. Not how to not work or where to draw the line. But how to work in a way that is clear—a way of working that allows me to stay committed to my practice, my family, and my business.

---

[*] See Nicole's full reflection in the appendix.

I'm always inspired by this list by Peter Fischli and David Weiss:

HOW to WORK BetteR

1. DO ONE tHiNG At A time
2. KNOW tHe PROBLeM
3. LeARN to LisTeN
4. LEARN to ASK qUeStioNS
5. DistiNGUisH seNSe fROM NONSeNSe
6. AccePt cHANGe AS iNeViTABle
7. Admit MistAKes
8. SAy it siMPle
9. Be CALM
10. sMile

CHAPTER 4 EXERCISE

Symbols are important and an easy way for us to tap into our deeper truths and desires. Find an oracle or a tarot deck that speaks to you. Also feel free to make your own: take a bunch of notecards and write words you love on them or collage images that are inspiring to you.

I love the Road to Nowhere Oracle Deck by Spirit Speak and the Aquarian Tarot Deck.

A daily task for me is drawing one of those cards. Before I read the booklet that explains each card, I ask myself what I see—what story is coming up for me and what messages are in it.

You can have a notebook where you write down your findings each day. Pay attention to what shows up more than once. Also consider the following:

- Do you sometimes make money from your hobbies?
- How does your relationship to social media sharing intersect with how you make money?
- What private tasks/hobbies/spiritual practices do you do for yourself that no one else knows about or sees?

CHAPTER 5

HOW to NOt WORK WHEN NOt WORKING

What does not working *really* look like?

People who take my workshops or know about this project generally ask me, "Well, Marlee, what IS THE ANSWER to how to not always be working?" Spoiler alert: If I were to really boil it down, this book could have been a one-page pamphlet saying, "Turn your phone off and go outside and never tell anyone you did it."

This could be oversimplifying things. If you are an herbalist, being outside and foraging wild plants is indeed your work. But it's the spirit of the idea: when your phone is turned off, even if you're working, you're connecting with the world, not digitally watching it. When I am dancing, I do not feel like I am working, even if I'm being paid. When I am answering emails about scheduling a dance workshop, it definitely feels like work even if I'm not being paid.

So identifying the parts of our work that don't *feel* like work, those gray areas, and honoring them is special. And remembering to go outside and not document every moment has been, for me, the key to not burning out and not always working.

A large part of my ability to cut down on working has come from understanding my addiction to my phone. Yes, I said it: addiction to the phone. Escapism through the phone.

Sometimes the phone is a way to obsess over my work. Sometimes the phone is a way to connect to my work. Sometimes the phone is a way to escape from whatever inner creative personal turmoil I am experiencing, to dive into a world that is not my real life.

The phone relationship appears a number of times in this book. It's a relationship I honestly wish I didn't have to write about and could be like, *Listen, y'all, I solved it, I am fine, I just LOVE MY LIFE so much that I NEVER want to look at my phone.*

Sometimes this is true. But I continue to find that my phone creeps in at unexpected times and in furiously annoying and disconnecting ways.

Here are a few things I have tried, and am trying, to be mindful of in my relationship to my phone.

○ ○ ○

WAYS I HAVE TRIED TO OVERCOME PHONE ADDICTION

GET RID OF APPS No apps. Delete all apps. Even if it's just for the day. Or for a week.

Do not have a Facebook app on the phone. You truly do not need this. You might want it, but let Facebook be the *one* social media *thing* you just do on a damn computer. Let's collectively allow ourselves the time and space to *wait* and do the thing later.

A note on apps and travel: Sometimes it is better to work smarter, not harder, when you are traveling. If this is the case, by all means have the Facebook app on your phone. But if you are experiencing a typical workweek with access to your browser, I would say delete the app.

A NOTE ON WEATHER AND MAPS Geoffrey Holstad, a designer at Patagonia, facilitator of Cabin-Time creative residency, and deep inspirational friend, suggested to me to have only the weather app and Google Maps available—so if you want a *true* social media detox, this is an option.

A FLIP PHONE I did this, I loved it. I did this, I hated it. Where to even begin with the flip phone . . .

The formula I used was to get a flip phone, a straight-up T9-texting forty-dollar flip phone, but to keep my deactivated iPhone as basically a Wi-Fi machine/iPod/tablet, which I needed for my business. So, you see, I still had the capabilities of a full iPhone, only now I was managing two devices.

This was not an improvement. It felt like I added to the chaos rather than subtracted from it. I also honestly did not realize how often I text my friends near and far. When I switched to T9 from the fluid and powerful ways of iMessage (both its quick-typing magic *and* the actual *language* that is emojis), I became really stunted in my communication.

How can you love a thing that seems to be ripping you from the world? How can you let that thing pull you in in a tender and loving way? How can you talk about it without feeling like you've officially lost your mind? The realization that my phone was also helping me connect as much as it was isolating me was the beginning of a healing path to my iPhone.

In the end, I switched back to simply having an iPhone. I truly found that carrying two devices was an even *bigger* distraction than just having one. If I had been able to set up a world where

I never needed or wanted technology at my fingertips, maybe it could have worked. But the reality is that ignoring your phone in a world where everyone has one is not a good solution. So I try to return to the *feeling* of a flip phone—of slowing down and having a limited range of options—as often as I can. It got me to start carrying around a disposable camera (which I still do) as a way of documenting my life and friends without having to take my phone out every two minutes. I really enjoyed the separate devices: one for photographing and one for communicating. I try to still practice that when it makes sense.

PHONE BOX This is an idea borrowed from my incredible friend and publisher Caroline Paquita.

Get a box. It can be really simple. A shoebox works, but it's fun to get like a *really* beautiful wooden box or a plain box that you collage or paint or something. Make it a temple. Not a temple for the phone, but a temple for your *spirit,* which will have a lighter load upon using the phone box.

You decide how long you'd like to *not* look at your phone. I like to go longer than feels comfortable. Let's start with three hours. It's okay if you've literally never gone three hours without looking at your phone. Let's try it.

Put the phone in the phone box. Now go do something: work, write, walk, all of the above. Whatever makes you feel alive. Use it as a break from talking to people. You don't have to have a real or deep or meaningful reason for using the phone box. When it's time, it's time. Or when it doesn't feel like it's time, this could also be a really great time.

Stick to your time. Don't take the phone out of the box until it is time to take the phone out of the box.

This in many ways reminds me of the Miranda July short film "A Handy Tip for the Easily Distracted," where she puts all of her technology under bowls and then holds a white dress she loves hostage by placing a shallow pan of grape juice on it. It might feel wild to have come so far that you need a box. This is okay. This is okay. This is the world we live in, and it's okay to need a box for your phone.

App Suggestions

It might seem counterintuitive to use an app to moderate your phone usage, but these are some I have found to be useful:

MOMENT Moment is a free app that tracks your screen time, how many times you pick up your phone in a day, and how much time you spend using each app. It's terrifying. And it's totally beautiful. It can be really surprising to see how many *hours* a bunch of five-minute scrolls and two-minute texting bouts add up to. You get to set your goal for how much screen time you'd like to use in a day, and it makes you a nice chart so that you can see if you've gone over or not. Green for great job, yellow for close, and red for going over. Do you go on red *every single day*? That's okay, but maybe make your screen time allowance bigger and work down from there. Let yourself see some green.

It's not meant to punish you. It's meant to be information. This is all just information. What you do with it is a process and it is gentle and it is soft and it is okay if some days you hit six hours. Or maybe that's a lot, but maybe that day you wrote a book on your phone.

Navigating *all* of this is so incredibly personal. But if you are really struggling that is okay.

FREEDOM This is another app where you can have a free trial (again, lots of free options—but this could be good for some). You can block apps from your phone for anywhere from an hour to twenty-four hours! Super helpful. It also blocks you from going into your phone web browser. Because we have all had that moment when we've deleted an app and then just gone to its website . . .

SELFCONTROL This is an app for your computer (available at self-controlapp.com), and it has been my go-to for almost a decade. SelfControl lets you make a list of websites you don't want to be able to access on your computer while you are working, like seriously blocks you so hard. It feels great to know I can be working in Google Docs and Gmail but have no access to Tumblr, Pinterest, Twitter, Instagram, Facebook, etc.

This one feels especially important, because even when I get my phone out of the room or turn it off, I often have so many emails and so much writing to do that they weigh on me and I wind up distracting myself online. I think sometimes I get afraid I will just get sucked into an internet vortex, so I don't even want to try to sit down and work. Remember Roger from earlier in the book? That inner voice that tells me I will fail before I even start based on previous experiences of failing often? This is usually the moment he makes a grand entrance.

ROGER IS NOT RIGHT. Knowing these distractions are blocked makes it easier to try again *and* put Roger in his place. Thank the inner voice for its noticing of your patterns, download this free tool, and show up in a better and brighter way.

TURN IT OFF The app that came before all others—the off button.

Seriously, just turn your phone off. It will feel great.

Better yet, turn it off and put it in your car in the driveway.

WORDS ON UNPLUGGING BY
SARAH SCHULWEIS, BUSINESS CONSULTANT

I love that technology has given me the safety of the written word, as my introversion is an asset and a frustration. When I have a chance to express myself or touch base with a friend to tell them I love them via email or text, it gives me the chance to connect while protecting my limited extroverted energy.

So how to unplug? Literally the off button.

Our best work as creatives—big-picture thinking, creativity, strategy, ideas, connection—can only happen when stepping away. Sure, I've had weeks that felt nonstop, but I savor the days, weeks, months when balance feels like the priority.

I leave it (my phone) in the other room or off my body as much as I can. I take walks without it. I turn it off completely when I walk into therapy, dinners with friends, or whenever my attention needs to be on anything but my phone.

I make it harder to sign in to addictive apps.

I make sure that my clients and friends know that reaching me and getting a response could take some time, but that I love and care for them.

Overall, technology is my most coveted tool for work, and when I feel tired, frustrated, or have negative self-talk, I step away and connect with my actual inner thoughts.

AIRPLANE MODE When you sleep, when you don't want cellular waves coming.

STRICT PHONE HOURS Setting phone hours can empower you to actually love and honor your phone time. I let myself scroll the feed every day at one P.M. for twenty minutes.

That way you don't have to feel a weird and crazy guilt—you can just accept that it's scrolling time.

Also, you can set a "No Phone Before Ten A.M." rule or a phone curfew in the afternoons/evenings.

Play with it! There is no right way for everyone.

CHAPTER 5 EXERCISE

Below, write out answers to the following questions.

- What activities make you feel truly relaxed?
- What are action steps to creating clear boundaries around not working? (For instance, I put a basket of knitting next to my couch so that I can *always* reach for that instead of the phone or laptop.)
- How do you feel in your body when you are not working? How can you return to that feeling?
- What can you carry with you as tools to not work on a commute or when you know you'll have downtime away from home? (I started carrying a notebook and pens for drawing!)

_____

_____

_____

_____

_____

_____

_____

taking a break

Exploring the idea of a healthy break has become so important to me. It could look different for each individual person. Maybe a healthy break for you is going for a walk, while maybe someone else is writing a book about walking, so they need another outlet. A break could be making a meal, which to some people is a chore called "feeding yourself." But I know in my busy world of always wanting to *do, do, do*, sometimes the simple act of making a salad is the greatest gift of not working.

One of my favorite ways to take a break is stretching, light movement, and yoga. But, again, dancing and movement are in so, so many ways my work in this world. So here we are again, facing the deeply gray areas of the entire idea of this book.

But in terms of what feels like my career—writing books/teaching—I have found that movement without expectation (so not specifically tied to research and lesson planning) can be a freedom from working. Working in the job sense, that is.

Having a consistent movement practice, whether this is walking, dancing, yoga, or stretching, keeps us embodied and attached to our bodies. Being embodied is a way of staying attuned to ourselves, which keeps us available and in service to our communities.

Often when I work at home, the first things I do are to make sure I have a snack and to lay my yoga mat out. This way, when it is time to take a break, I am already held by the universe and prepared. In my tired state, I don't have to *think* about *if* I should roll out my yoga mat, because I've done it pre-work session. And when it is time to take a break, I can just step onto it.

Yoga has come in and out of my life in many ways, but even the smallest leap into this practice—child's pose or legs up the wall—can be incredibly grounding when I am all over the place.

The beauty of a practice of movement (or stillness) is that we learn to let our body be our anchor. Learning the language of sensation and what it means to honor ourselves as we explore our capacity comes with the territory. As we navigate the many layers of our experience, there's an opportunity to reclaim ourselves and make the shift from scattered to steady.

A major gift of practice is that as it deepens, answers to questions like "Is this right for me?" or "What do I need right now?" come more naturally, because we learn to move from the knowing of our bodies. It doesn't necessarily make things easy, but it does make things simple.

The tricky part about creating space to pause and practice is that at first it will need to be deliberate. It might even feel forced. Soon you'll start to taste the sweetness of it all, which comes from knowing that every time you choose to pause, you are choosing yourself.

—RACHELLE KNOWLES, YOGA TEACHER

SING. WRITE. PRAY.

by Brandi Harper, knitter

- I rise and drink water before scrolling through my phone.
- Then comes a cleanse with apple cider vinegar, lemon water, or kombucha.
- The morning begins with a smoothie for now and the making of a green juice for later.
- I choose three asanas and do them at home.
- I cook a meal three times a week.
- I practice hot yoga three times a week.
- I go on a date with myself once a month.
- Sing. Write. Pray. These can never happen often enough.
- And I'm honoring daily the neurosis of always doing things in threes.

CHAPTER 6 EXERCISE

Take out a separate piece of paper. Write down your answers to these questions. Tape them to your wall.

- What does a fifteen-minute break look like? Legs up the wall, a walk around the block, drinking a glass of water?
- What does an hour of not working look like?
- What does five hours of not working look like?
- Okay, here we go, what does one whole damn day of not working look like?
- What is a vacation?
- What is a work trip?
- Do I want work and vacation to be the same thing? (It's totally okay if you do, but I know I have gone on "work vacations" where I totally forgot to carve out non-work time, so then when I was actually taking a break, I just felt so guilty for not working!)

CHAPTER 7

tHeRe is No MeSSiNg UP; or, MY OWN PeRSoNAL MANifesto

just googled "there is no messing up" to see what would come up. An image of me making a dress appeared. It is of my feet, standing next to a dress pattern on the floor of my house in Michigan. It is of me sewing a dress for my wedding shower, a day that was nice for a marriage that did not last. It did not last, but it did not fail—it transformed into a new way of partnership.

There is no messing up; there is only shifting and rearranging.

This is an incredibly personal example, but it applies to many other aspects of my life.

A small instance of this is when I get behind on shipping. My web orders will be pouring in, I will forget to ask for help, and I will drown in deep judgment of self for not doing my job well. Alas, spiraling into a headspace of "Wow, I've really messed up" doesn't really help to solve the problem. There is shifting, there is rearranging. There is informing. Most of the time when I get behind in a way that demands an apology, amends, or business recourse, I can simply send an email telling a customer or client exactly what is happening: making sense of my mess rather than just ignoring it/hoping it goes away.

I think that's part of how we heal from being so afraid to mess up or of when something gets clunky. Just being hopeful that a tricky situation will disappear does not in fact work. We have to be honest and open and willing to create clarity where there is vagueness.

On a larger scale, on May 17, 2011, I quit drinking. As I write this book, it's been six and a half years since I've taken a drink. While I commit to this task for only twenty-four hours at a time, by the time you read this it may still be true. If it is not, it will have become a new truth. When I look back at the first half of 2011, it feels like a real mess-up. But when I think of every moment that brought me here to write thesepages, there really, really is no messing up.

I haven't done much with manifestos myself in long form, but I feel like every day I give myself a little *boost* or a little *yes* that takes me far. This boost can come from anywhere. For me, sometimes

I'll pull an oracle card from the deck before writing my morning pages and then use it to write a sentence or two.

If I pull the birth card, I can write:

Today I will birth all that is new.
Today I will birth myself, I will hold myself.
Today I will birth old ideas and new ones.

Or if I pick the water card, it can be as simple as:

Today I am gonna drink a shit ton of water.

Your manifesto does not have to be spiritual or poetic, or it can be the most powerful poem you have ever written. Your manifesto can also be a to-do list about how you are going to love the grocery store.

Poet and friend Jacqueline Suskin is someone I have looked to for years for the tiniest manifestos. Part of her practice is performance poetry, writing on-the-spot improvised poems for people in real life at a party, the farmers' market, a baby shower. Here are some ways Jacqueline puts the manifesto into a Daily Ideal.

A DAILY IDEAL MANIFESTO
BY JACQUELINE SUSKIN

For years I've set aside time for retreats. I make a plan to leave my day-to-day life behind and go somewhere quiet, where I hardly know anyone. In solitude, I'm incredibly productive. During one of these retreats in Joshua Tree, I thought about my life in the city and asked myself: What would I do at home if I had an entire day of uninterrupted time? I filled up a page in my journal with various categories like spiritual practice, exercise, creative projects, and career outreach. Under these categories I made lists that helped clear up my priorities. I compiled all of these considerations into a page of guidelines that I like to call the Daily Ideal.

DAILY IDEAL

WAKE UP EARLY - TEA
STRETCH - ALTAR - TEA
WRITE - READ - EAT - WRITE
WORK - WALK - WORK - TEA
PLANS - FRIENDS - DANCE

ONCE A WEEK AT LEAST
OCEAN - FOREST - DESERT
10 A.M. - 10 P.M. PHONE RULES
10 A.M. - 3 P.M. DEEP FOCUS

NIGHTTIME HANG TIME
PRACTICE NO
EARLY to RISE. MORNING SOLITUDE AND QUIET
ALTAR TIME. HOT TEA, WRITING, TOAST, OATS, FRUIT...
TIME OUTSIDE, WALKING, STRETCHING, BEING...
WORK ON A SPECIFIC PROJECT FOR A DECENT AMOUNT
OF TIME, INTERNET TIME MINIMAL AND
RESEARCH BASED.
EAT GOOD MEALS; DRINK A LOT OF WATER AND TEA.
AT LEAST AN HOUR EVERY DAY READING A BOOK.
EXERCISE, YOGA, DANCE, BICYCLE, SWIMMING IS GOOD...
STUDY SOMETHING: LANGUAGE, ECOLOGY, HISTORY...
CONNECT WITH ONE FRIEND FRIEND IN A MEANINGFUL WAY.
ALTAR TIME AGAIN. EARLY to BED.

This is different from a to-do list or a timetable. The Daily Ideal is a reliable foundation that I always circle back to when I lose focus or get distracted. If I follow my own suggestions, I end up with a lifestyle that allows me to feel satisfied and productive.

In addition to the Daily Ideal, I love setting rules for myself and having some specific things that I won't compromise. For example, every morning and every night I sit at an altar and light a candle. The practice that occurs in front of the altar varies: I pray, I meditate, I breathe, I give thanks, I pull cards, I hold crystals and burn sage . . . However it goes, it happens morning and night no matter where I am or how tired I am. In the last five years, I've missed only a few sittings, and this dedication resets me, it grounds me and reminds me what I'm trying to do with my life; it clears my mind and brings me back to myself.

Here is where we get to really celebrate what we are doing that is worth high-fiving yourself for. Or, better yet, identifying what we want to strive to be. The only trick is there is no judgment allowed here, only noticing. So we can make some goals, some personal mantras, and a lengthy (or short, depending on your vibe) personal manifesto—but we do *not* get permission to hate ourselves for not "being where we wish we were." There just isn't room for that here. I mean, it will happen, the voice will pop up, but you can greet it and thank it and remind it you're doing just fine noticing and don't need to turn that work into judging.

CHAPTER 7 EXERCISES

HERE IS WHERE WE DIVE INTO THE PERSONAL MANIFESTO: What are powerful words you use to describe yourself? Make a list:

_____

_____

_____

_____

_____

_____

_____

Now take those words and turn them into li'l mantras (e.g., "I am healing," "I am powerful," "My place on this earth is important").

Now combine all your mantras into one personal manifesto.

○ ○ ○

EXERCISE ON
SHIFTING PERSPECTIVE

Below are some phrases I use to remind myself I can actively change my thinking, so when my brain's tiny negative voice tells me one thing, I can practice shifting the language. For instance, if a typical thought for you is "Wow, I missed that deadline, I am a dumb ass," you could instead say, "Welp, looks like I missed another deadline. That really seems to be a habit of mine. How can I support myself to meet the deadline, or at least love myself through the missing it? *Oh!* I will make myself tea, sit down, and finish it. Even if it is a few days late, it can still be special."

We spend so much time beating ourselves up, which rarely pushes us into deep or profound work.

A few suggestions for reframing negative thoughts to be powerful mini manifestos of not just self-love but also self-*esteem:*

- I am okay. I can do better next time. And even if I do the same thing a million times in a row, there is still room for me to change and shift.
- Messing up is part of being alive. Being alive is messy. If I notice where I "messed up" (we put this in quotes because remember: there is no messing up), then I can simply move on without judgment.
- I will make myself some tea or run myself a bath. I probably am overworked because I have not planned out enough time to rest.
- I will put my phone down now and take some deep breaths. I might just be forgetting to breathe and drink enough water.
- I will treat myself to something nice now, like a walk, a massage, a phone call with a friend.
- I will now be of service to another to release me from my self-damaging thoughts.

Now fill the spaces below with your own words:

When I overwork myself, instead of telling myself I did a bad job I can say:

_____

_____

_____

When I do a great job, I will tell myself (instead of "Well, it would have been nice if you would have done that sooner," etc.):

_____

_____

_____

When I miss a deadline, I can tell myself:

_____

_____

_____

When I dive into my phone for way longer than I meant to, I can tell myself:

_____

_____

_____

Use the space below to jot down other ways that you can practice self-acceptance:

_____

_____

_____

CHAPTER 8

ANxieties ANd feARS

ON COMPARISON TO OTHERS AND DOING ONE THING AT A TIME

It's easy to look around and think everyone else has it all figured out. You measure people's success by the number of followers they have, by the volume of stuff they appear to sell, by the photos they post of cool places they travel to. And regardless of any achievements you've made, you feel like you're just bumbling along making mistake after mistake, digging yourself into a hole you'll never find your way out of. But even the most seemingly successful of us have days filled with complete dread for all the tasks left undone, thinking of all the people who will soon find out we're a complete fraud—that we are actually making it all up as we go and are making many mistakes along the way. It's easy to get completely overwhelmed with the many jobs of running a small business, while also being a human. It's easy to feel like suddenly those emails left unopened are going to completely destroy you. But they're not. You know they're not. You just have to take a deep breath and remember: you are not alone. We're all stumbling sometimes, and the internet isn't real.

Then sit down and make a to-do list. Include tasks like "go for a walk" and "eat lunch," and start crossing things off, one at a time.

—ASHLEY BROWN DURAND,
OWNER OF SECRET HOLIDAY & CO.

Adrenal Fatigue and General Anxiety

A huge part of how I treat my anxiety is to nourish myself with herbal infusions. I am by no means an herbalist, but I have been lucky enough to be given access to this information in my community and would love to share.

There are many different ways to ingest herbs; the most common might be drinking tea!

Chamomile tea while journaling and reading before bed (phone off) is possibly my favorite way to not be working right up till I close my eyes. My body has a chance to wind down and I can find rest.

I was introduced to Susun Weed's nourishing herbal infusions by my mentor in Michigan. Below are my two favorites, but I would also suggest comfrey, linden flower, and red clover. Look up Susun Weed for a more in-depth look and access to her wealth of knowledge.

Nettle

Nettle infusion is my absolute favorite drink to put in my body.

When our adrenals are fatigued, we can feel sudden panic, fear, and anxiety. Nettle is amazing at calming and restoring the depleted adrenals and giving power and light to our insides. This infusion is what allows me to work really long days and not be totally exhausted and depleted. Nettle teaches me to listen to my body and know when it is time to rest. Nettle is important to me right before I travel or am going to be bouncing all over the place. Nettle also helps me with my sleep: I am ready for bed when it is time for bed and ready to rise upon waking.

Oatstraw

Oatstraw nourishes and tonifies the nervous system, and it is beneficial for your teeth and bones. This one is great for me when I know I am about to be around a bunch of people and need extra protection. Oatstraw is an incredibly calming herb. Also good for folks who experience anxiety mixed with excessive energy bursts (hello, me).

TO MAKE AN INFUSION Place 1 ounce of either herb in a quart-sized mason jar, fill the jar with boiling water, screw on the top, and let sit for four to eight hours. Strain the infusion and drink!

It is truly this simple. And like so many new tasks offered in this book, you can turn it into your own ritual! I love to put water on the stove to boil just as I am winding down for bed. I measure out my herbs, get my pajamas on, brush my teeth, get ready for the next day, pour my water on my herbs, and set my alarm. When I rise eight hours later, straining my infusion is part of my morning practice.

This practice is not only for me but for everyone I work with and am in relationship to, both on the internet and in my real life. When I am in crowds, my anxiety can flare up in a way that is really wild, so it is imperative, for my availability to the *work* of my life, to be nourished.

So, you see, this routine is about working. It's about being able to show up to my work in a clear and focused way so that I am not wildly scattered and unable to focus.

Tinctures

One of my go-tos for my morning routine and as an herbal medicine is lemon balm in tincture form. Half a dropper of lemon balm in a small glass of water in the morning eases the part of my anxiety that says, "Welp, good morning, today is doomed because you pretty much mess up every day." It eases my nervous system in a way that lets me approach the day gently.

I also love Sister Spinster's Devotion essence. Conjured up by Northern California herbalist Liz Migliorelli, this formula—with essences of blackberry, poppy, and pomegranate—is designed to stimulate creativity and help with self-realization. This essence has been hugely beneficial to me when I am looking to integrate new habits and new routines into my life.

Fear That There Is No Room for You in the Universe/ Creative World

This is just simply untrue. We need you. Moving on.

Anxiety Around Not Having Enough Time

I feel this so deeply. There are so many projects I truly want to do, and I am terrified I will waste so much time doing the "wrong things" or not being focused enough or . . . How many "enoughs" can I write here? Here is a little exercise:

WRITE OUT YOUR DREAM PROJECTS.

⦾ Number them in the order you'd like to get them done.

_____

_____

_____

_____

_____

⦾ Now pick two or three and use this space to make a timeline of when you would like to complete them:

_____

_____

_____

_____

_____

⊙ Okay, now that you have a timeline, what action steps can you take to make them happen?

_____

_____

_____

_____

_____

_____

Financial Fear

I am no expert at any of this. Ultimately, I have found that when I am *incredibly clear* on my finances—what is going out and what is coming in—then I have the *freedom* to make clearer decisions and not overwork. So often when the exhaustion of work comes up for me, it's because I am scared about money. Did I overspend on something this month? How much is coming in? Is enough ever *really* enough?

I have found that asking for help here is *huge, huge, huge*. I still mess this up all the time. My relationship to abundance is a whole other book and conversation, in terms of where I came from with money, my relationship to spending it addictively, and my tendency to be incredibly vague.

Don't be vague with how you spend money.

I think this is my greatest "advice." Not because I am perfect at it, but again because I know that when I am not vague with my relationship to money and spending, both personally and on a business level, I can start to see what's happening when and where. I can *notice it*.

We are vague because we are scared. And it's okay to be afraid; money is energy and there is so, so much wrapped up into it.

But I find that when I am being vague and not looking at the facts, I tend to overwork or stress or get really anxious, instead of just calmly looking at the numbers and thinking, "Okay, I need to make X amount of more dollars this month to cover my basic needs, and if I want to exceed that I have to teach X amount of classes, etc., etc."

Anxiety and fear keep us alive—as humans and as artists. I like to look at emotions head-on and figure out why I feel them and where those feelings are coming from. Healthy anxiety can keep you present and focused. Fear is an indicator of change. I don't tackle, I hold their hands.

by Sarah Schulweis, business consultant

CHAPTER 9

it's lighter than you think

Something to expand on is the truest joys of just being alive. Reading this book can feel like work. Working on yourself can feel like so much work that giving up feels like the least amount of work, so let's do that. But it is all so, so much lighter than we think, this whole being alive thing. How do we manage and maintain this lightness?

Non-Isolation: Being with Friends

I find that a lot of my inner pain around my work and creativity comes when I am in isolation—not to be confused with alone time; I love and cherish my alone time. But there is something about isolation that is different. It is about hiding, about not being witnessed. When we bear witness to ourselves and others and let them hold space for us, we can break open.

Engaging in Song and Dance

Like literally stop whatever you are doing and put on your favorite song. Sing in the car, in the shower. You do not have to be good at singing to sing (or at least I hope not, because I am very bad and love singing along).

And dancing! I might have a college degree in dance, but dancing is *of my being* in every way and has been since I was born. And I really believe it is in all of us. Just dance around your house. Maybe even do it naked, or put your favorite outfit on. It tricks you into feeling better before you even realize it.

Writing Gratitude Lists

This always keeps me light, keeps me humble, keeps me in service to my community. This shifts my perspective almost immediately. I am like, "Wow, yes, I have so much magic in my life." The sun, the moon, my family, coffee, swimming, baths, tattoos—the lists can change every day. Try making one *every single day* in your planner or somewhere easy to just always do it, even if you're writing down only one thing.

Reaching Out, Asking for Help

Ask your friends for help and let them be there for you. And then when it is time to switch, be there for them. One beautiful way to keep things light and get out of my own head is to call or text a friend and just ask how they are, offer them a five-minute phone call to vent or celebrate or share. Nine out of ten times they are like, "Whoa, yes, I miss you and needed you in this moment!" Listening to them and being there for them usually gets me out of my own shit pretty fast.

Support Groups: Therapy, Sharing Circles

Keeping it light, which is often just about a perspective shift, is hard to do alone. I have found that twelve-step groups, new moon circles, book clubs, knitting groups, and other community-oriented gatherings keep me *right-sized.* They keep me in a place of steadiness, a spot I often get knocked off of.

> You are not alone, you never have been,
> and you never will be.

All of these exercises and ideas are brought to you from my own brain. They are all things I am not an expert at, and I am still learning all the ways to not always be working. As I wrote this book I think what I really did discover is: *It's all work, always.* So it's not about never working or working less or making no money or getting rich. What I am attempting to research and discover is how to forgive myself when I become undisciplined and how to keep trying when I make a mistake or don't meet my own expectations.

Much of my own research for this book is drawn from Sister Corita Kent's rules for the classroom:

IMMACULATE HEART COLLEGE ART DEPARTMENT RULES

RULE 1. FIND A PLACE YOU TRUST AND THEN TRY
TRUSTING IT FOR A WHILE.

RULE 2. GENERAL DUTIES OF A STUDENT:
PULL EVERYTHING OUT OF YOUR TEACHER.
PULL EVERYTHING OUT OF YOUR FELLOW STUDENTS.

RULE 3. GENERAL DUTIES OF A TEACHER:
PULL EVERYTHING OUT OF YOUR STUDENTS.

RULE 4. CONSIDER EVERYTHING AN EXPERIMENT.

RULE 5. BE SELF-DISCIPLINED. THIS MEANS FINDING
SOMEONE WISE OR SMART AND CHOOSING
TO FOLLOW THEM. TO BE DISCIPLINED IS TO
FOLLOW IN A GOOD WAY. TO BE SELF-DISCIPLINED
IS TO FOLLOW IN A BETTER WAY.

Rule 6. Nothing is a mistake. There's no win and no fail. There's only make.

Rule 7. The only Rule is work. If you work it will lead to something. Its the people who do all of the work all of the time who eventually catch on to things.

Rule 8. Don't try to create and analyze at the same time. They're different processes.

Rule 9. Be happy whenever you can manage it. Enjoy yourself. It's lighter than you think.

Rule 10. "We're breaking all of the rules. Even our own rules. And how do we do that? By leaving plenty of room for X quantities."
        John Cage

Helpful hints: Always be around. Come or go to everything. Always go to classes.

Read anything you can get your hands on.
Look at movies carefully, often.
Save everything — it might come in handy later.

There should be new rules next week.

More from Jacqueline Suskin:

Another system that really helps is setting time frames. When I'm working on a writing project I make a weekly schedule. For a while now it's looked something like this: Monday is my day off to take lunch meetings/hold office hours. Tuesday through Friday I try to work on writing until at least three P.M., and then from three to five P.M. I'll do emails and more business-oriented work. I like to save administrative stuff for the later part of the day and use my fresh morning brain for creative focus. In the evenings I'll see friends, go to shows, or even have some late meetings. I usually have gigs on the weekends, but any other time off on weekends is free time, and I make sure I go to the beach or the forest at least once. This schedule allows me to balance my creative practice, my job outreach/management, and my free time in a way that is really fulfilling.

To follow these rules that I make for myself I have to remember two really important things:

1 I HAVE TO BE FLEXIBLE. I cannot be insanely rigid and creative at the same time. Some days I don't have it in me to keep a perfect routine. I need to wrap up early and go for a walk, pick my friend up at the airport, or get an ice-cream cone. It's hard work to be my own boss and sometimes it's even harder to let myself off the hook. Everything is adjustable and I continue to learn how empowering it can be to go easy on myself.

2 **I HAVE TO PRACTICE SAYING NO.** I am such a YES person! I want to do it all, try everything, and give each option its fair chance, but it's just not possible! Learning how to say no has been a beautiful challenge for me. Of course it's a balance, but by saying no I end up doing better work, I spend more time on the Daily Ideal and ultimately feel better about my quality of life because I'm not spread too thin. Saying no also leaves room for me to say yes to things that I wouldn't have time for otherwise, like dancing, sitting and staring at the horizon, talking to my cat, reading tons of poetry, taking long baths, climbing trees, going to the movies, going on walks without a destination, etc.

These commitments require endless revisions and work well for me because I listen to myself. If something is off with my productivity or I'm feeling dissatisfied, I check in to see what I can adjust. Maybe I need to take a week off and go on an impromptu retreat. Maybe I need to collaborate with a friend because I'm feeling isolated. Maybe I need to write poems all night instead of waking up early and going to the market. Maybe I need to focus on business outreach and line up jobs because I'm stressed about money. When I listen to myself and follow my own needs, I end up balancing out the various types of work and expression that make my life so magical.

○ ○ ○

A lot of this book has been me guessing, me attempting to share what I have figured out, sometimes on my own and many times in a group. I have hosted How to Not Always Be Working workshops all over the country for a variety of people. The biggest thing that seems to come out is: do something sweet for someone and don't tell anyone you did it.

Privacy, tenderness, what we keep for ourselves—these grow more and more scarce every day. The more feeds we have to post on and the more gadgets we have to document with, the harder it becomes to keep things sacred.

This also goes for our land, for our hearts, for our communities.

We put such an incredible pressure on ourselves, and in this time of technology, that pressure can increase in a way that is wildly destructive to our hearts, minds, and creative practices.

Comparison seems to be more and more built into our psyche. We spend so much time consuming the work of others that we assume there is nothing left for us—why make an offering when everyone else already is?

Because it's light, because it's fun, because it is *your divine responsibility* to the world to share your work with it.

Our work is whatever we say it is. Our work is to be of service, to give back, to lift up our voices (and be quiet and lift up others when they need it).

How to Not Always Be Working is not about not working. It isn't about the four-hour workweek or finding some sort of deep balance.

How to Not Always Be Working is about noticing. It's about paying deep attention to every moment, every person, and every gift you are being given.

It's about the choice we all have to break open and access freedom and creativity.

It's about eye contact and touch.

It's about feet in dirt and plants.

It's about dancing and singing.

It's about being a good friend.

It's about all the things you wouldn't give a second thought to if you knew you would die in five hours.

If you would have called your dad back or sent your mom that email.

Or kissed your dog and told it you loved it.

Or texted your friend.

It's about loving your work so much that you can step away from it (it needs space sometimes too).

It's about loving being alive so much that you can step back and say, "Yes, this is what I want to be paying attention to." And no matter what your profession or task or job is, you are the boss of your body and you are the boss of those decisions.

I do not fully understand this yet, but it felt time to expand, to tell you what I know. To tell you how I have been putting in the work to not always be working, to reimagine my life in a way where I can put my phone away at the dinner table and taste my food.

To not text while I am driving so I see a baby calf being born.

To have time to return a phone call.

To remind myself that we get this body only once, so showing up all the way is going to be necessary.

Grateful to be alive today.

Grateful to share these words today.

xo

ACKNOWLEDGMENTS

This page is a love letter of gratitude to the amazing team of humans who made this book possible

My agent Kate Woodrow and my editor Emma Brodie, there are hardly words in the English dictionary for how lucky I am to have you both in my life

Kate found the zine version of this book at Case For Making in San Francisco in 2015, she believed in it, helped me build it from a few typewritten pages to a full book vision, and she has been my biggest cheerleader since the beginning.

Emma took a google doc filled with run on sentences and vague ideas and sculpted them into a real book that makes sense. She made sure we got to keep the word witch and talk about class, capitalism, and prayer. She is the grit behind my softness.

To Rob, who drew this book and joined me in a process of trusting our timeline, of everlasting friendship, who sees the world as earth and clouds and water.

To the radical women of Morrow: Liate Stehlik, Lynn Grady, Cassie Jones, Susan Kosko, Leah Carlson-Stanisic, Alicia Tatone, Andrea Molitor, Molly Waxman, and Jessica Lyons.

And to Nickey, my employee, best friend, collaborator, you are the person who knows my work, pushes me, tells me the truth, and sat next to me while I wrote most of this book. Thank you, I love you.

APPENDIX

At the Cracker Barrel in Tewksbury, Massachusetts
by Angel Nafis

I already know how real the tip will be for the Black
waitress. Her name is Asia. We are the only ones in this
restaurant that is half diner half gift-shop where it is
Christmas in October. I ask *what's really good here?*
I mean, really. She lowers her voice and says
I just started working here myself, there's not too
much I really mess with, but, the mash potatoes are good,
people seem to really like the chicken fried chicken.
I order just that plus Mac'n'Cheese and a hot black tea.
My bottom lip stains the mug a MAC Dusty Plum
and I already know here comes the poem. I am too
Woo-Woo, too my father's daughter to keep
what is mine to me so here I go. Tell her about
the couple dozen brown and black high schoolers
at the hotel across the way, how I have been brought
to read them poems for a *Diversity Retreat.*
She says *Oh? That's cool.* Brings me extra honey.
New England is in full swing. Stank maples release

their feral reds and yellows electric with every coax
of the wind and I feel farther from Michigan than I have
ever been. So when business picks up and she says
I'm not gonna disappear on you, I am relieved
Tewksbury saw fit I get me a sister solid. She
goes to the other tables where white folks fold
napkins crisp on white laps. I hear her tell them
her name, it is not our little secret. Asia is just
at work. But *Mashallah,* I am at work too. I know we
aren't blood, but she said she don't eat pork either and so
recommends the brown gravy. This is a high-key act of love
in a town no bigger than my thumb where Dolly Parton CD
signs swing brazen above the Hershey displays.
I don't want to throw all my cards on the table but
somebody is looking out. Mom's bones in the ground,
but O, my life, the harvest. So I wring the rag out
wherever I go. I part the curtains. I lather on the day.
Each alarm a voice saying, if you here, I'm here.
Back home, the blue-black train conductor who winks
at me and holds the doors an extra twenty seconds.
The chestnut banker, who despite her pinstripes
snickers at my jokes, circles her name on the
card she hands me. That mailman with the locks,
who made room for me on the sidewalk and said
I'm not tryna bother you, I don't want to scare
you, but you are really something.
These ramshackle angels, Sprawling,
anonymous, Woo-Woo, right on time.

The Fair
by Nicole Lavelle

It is difficult to be present completely. I find it rare that a leisure experience encompasses my attention, takes me entirely, is able to keep me from having planning thoughts or future-worry.

The fair[*] is an exception. The fair is an encompassing experience. For me, there is a shift that happens as soon as I am finished purchasing my ticket from the person in the plywood kiosk and I step through the chain-link fence into a dusty, crowded fairgrounds in the summer.

The fair is overstimulating in the best way. It requires my entire attention span. It requires me to be present.

The optical deluge of kitsch, vernacular signage, and attention-grabbing gestures is wild. Pushing through the smells and sounds to navigate through space is an exercise that takes great focus, even if I'm just trying to wander, amble, browse. There is a lot. It is enough to scramble me, but if I decide to ride the wave I just might achieve some kind of mental refresh, some kind of major palate-cleansing distraction. Sometimes it's helpful to get scrambled.

The fair is a social form with a deep history, a gathering propelled by competition and spectacle that is a weird microcosm of American culture. Some ingredients are consistently on display: award ribbons pinned to cages of living and breathing agriculture, displays of industrial innovation, live technology demos narrated by a guy with a headset mic, unreasonably fried food, bands that are a little past their prime, death-trap rides where the fear comes not from heights or speed but a concern for the soundness of the rusty bolts and old safety straps . . .

---

[*] When I say "fair," I mostly mean the county fair or the state fair that comes around once a year. Some other things that might fit with what I'm talking about: rodeos, country fairs, Renaissance fairs, town festivals . . .

One of my favorite parts is that each fair has a little regional flavor that sites me exactly where I am, in small-town Oregon or the urban South or the affluent Bay Area. This regional distinction is the strongest in the arts and crafts zone, usually found indoors in large halls (near the bathrooms, so, you know, I gotta go there anyway). Perched on display atop white plinths and black tablecloths are quilts, cakes, paintings, dioramas, needlepoint, baskets, lace, flower arrangements, jams, jellies, pickles, sculptures made of foam, furniture made of wood, amateur history displays. The regionally specific clues are often subtle, but they're there: organic hand soap in the bathrooms and distilled water spigots for your reusable bottles (Marin), a third-place ribbon on a Lego sculpture in the shape of a Confederate flag (Raleigh), or vaguely hippie burritos at the food court (Eugene).

Sometimes there is bingo. Sometimes there are fireworks. I always try to stand in line for at least one ride.

The fair puts contemporary culture on display. It is a sampling. It makes me think about a lot of important things at once, and somehow none of the pressing important things lingering on my to-do list. Email does not exist at the fair. It is one of my favorite ways to exist in one moment. I can't ignore the throngs of summer humans or the huge stuffed poop emoji hanging overhead. I can't tune out the slow drawl of the man announcing flavors of pie over the PA or the screams of joyful terror as the Scrambler rolls around again.

Thank you to my amazing contributors who shared their thoughts on work and paying deep attention.

Angel Nafis—http://www.angelnafis.com/
Sarah Schulweis—http://www.anchorandorbit.com/
Josey Baker—http://www.joseybakerbread.com/
Ashley Brown Durand—http://shop.secretholidayco.com/
Brandi Harper—http://www.purlbknit.com/
Rachelle Knowles—http://www.rachelleknowles.com/
Nicole Lavelle—http://www.nicolelavelle.com/
Jacqueline Suskin—http://www.yoursubjectyourprice.com

Websites of other names noted in this book

Geoffrey Holstad—http://geoffreyholstad.com/
Caroline Paquita—http://www.carolinepaquita.com/
Julia Cameron—http://juliacameronlive.com/
Angeles Arrien—http://www.angelesarrien.com/
Megan—Adventure Textiles—http://www.adventuretextiles.com/
Liz Migliorelli—Sister Spinster—http://www.sisterspinster.net/
Mary Evans—Spirit Speak—https://www.spirit-speak.com/
Adrienne Maree Brown—http://adriennemareebrown.net/
Eva Hoffman—http://www.identitytheory.com/eva-hoffman/